O'KEEFFE

Her robe is a cloud, her face a flower;
Her balcony, glimmering with bright spring dew,
Is either the tip of earth's Jade Mountain
Or a moon-edged roof of paradise.

Li Po

from *Jade Mountain*
(translated by Witter Bynner)

O'Keeffe

◦: DAYS IN A LIFE :◦

C. S. Merrill

University of New Mexico Press • Albuquerque

University of New Mexico Press edition published 2014 by arrangement with the author.

Printed in the United States of America

21 20 19 18 17 16   2 3 4 5 6 7

Library of Congress Cataloging-in-Publication Data

Merrill, C. S. (Carol S.)
  [Poems. Selections]
  O'Keeffe : days in a life / C.S. Merrill. — University of New Mexico Press edition.
    pages cm
  ISBN 978-0-8263-5420-4 (paper : alk. paper) — ISBN 978-0-8263-5421-1 (electronic)
  1. O'Keeffe, Georgia, 1887–1986—Poetry. 2. American poetry—20th century. I. Title.
  PS3563.E745163O34 2014
  811'.54—dc23
                              2013042820

Thank you to the Witter Bynner Foundation for Poetry, Inc. for an individual
poet's grant in 1994, to complete the manuscript for this book.

Thank you to the following people who critiqued the final stages of the manuscript:
Jimmy Santiago Baca   John Brandi
Hathaway Barry   Allen Ginsberg
Ross Lockridge   Pita Lopez
Dr. Harold Martin   Laura McGowan
Dr. Allen Minge   Anna Ortega
Avis Vermilye   Edith Wylder

Thank you to people who have inspired and encouraged me during the years of writing
this book:
  Theo Abel, Kazuko Asaba, Sabra Jane Basler, Noël Bennett, Dorie Bunting, Maria
  Chabot, Dr. Jock Cobb, Holly Cobb, David Gilmore, Merton Gilmore, Niki Glen, Joy
  Harjo, Harmon Houghton, Dr. John Howarth, Vivian Ivey, Betty Johnson, Pat Jojola,
  Edith Kent, Dale Kessinger, Richard Levine, Liu Siong, Elma Martin, James Moore, Ann
  Murray, Dr. Suzann Owings, Kip Powell, Joseph Rael, Marilyn Reeders, Bob and Melanie
  Sachs, Nanao Sakaki, Pete Smith, Karen Stone, Frank Trainer, Martha Trainer, Mona
  Wilgus, and Xu Xiao-wen.

Cover and text design by J. B. Bryan

Deep thanks to my parents:
Paul and Louise Merrill
for giving me life

Thanks to
Grandmothers and Grandfathers

Loving thanks to my son
Issa Abraham Sakaki Merrill
for seeing the truth of things

O'Keeffe answered my letter. I first visited her one day in August 1973. She hired me to work on weekends as librarian, secretary, cook, nurse, or companion from 1973 to 1979. This poetry is from my journals written a few hours after the experiences.

O'Keeffe did not like poetry. However, she would listen to Witter Bynner's translations of Chinese poets in *Jade Mountain*. O'Keeffe often had me read aloud to her from biographies of the great. Many times we re-read an ancient Taoist text *Secret of the Golden Flower*.

O'Keeffe taught me to cook. She taught me to look, really look, at things. She showed me how to live. She let me know her when she faced old age, blindness, and death in the last years of her life.

O'Keeffe must be remembered. She was a woman of fierce temper, infinite kindness, and impeccable sense of artistry. She encouraged me and changed my life.

I like to think of her walking in beauty beneath ancient cliffs at Ghost Ranch. This work is thanks for the strength of her will and the spirit of her work.

C. S. Merrill
September, 1995

1

The roofless room with vigas and screen
two gigantic jade trees in pots.
Against the far wall a slight niche
with a huge black rock there.
On the whole white wall, a slight shadow
and that rock. O'Keeffe's sight so poor
she doesn't see it, but knows it's there.
Also one moonflower plant blooming wide open
and onions drying on screens, fragrance of earth.

August, 1973

2

O'Keeffe at lunch, the table her design
patty pan squash & zucchini lightly steamed
carrots cooked in butter & dill;
home-baked bread with sunflower seeds
thinly sliced roast beef, chipped ice in glasses
with raspberry juice and mint tea.
In the center a large glass bowl
with an enormous pink hibiscus flower
floating with a green sprig of tansy
"good for a miscarriage," O'Keeffe said
talking of herbs for female parts.
In the roofless room trumpet flower blooming.

August, 1973

3

O'Keeffe used to go
to the Lawrence Ranch
before Frieda died.
Trees have grown
and the view is
not so full
as it used to be.
She used to rest
under one tree,
spent much time
looking up through branches
her head by the trunk.

August, 1973

4

O'Keeffe loved
a silk kimono
she wore so much
there was a hole
in the seat of it;
patched it
with a satin patch,
wore a hole
in that.
Couldn't bring herself
to patch the patch.
"You know…
glad we were young
when we were,
wouldn't want to be these days."

August, 1973

5

O'Keeffe lost her eyesight slowly
in a store in Santa Fe
walked out to a dim day
surprised the day was overcast.
Next day was overcast, but it wasn't;
that was how it started, a bloodclot
so she has to look to one side to see.

September, 1973

6

One worker came to the sliding door
long hair, mustache, and a little slumped
asked to trim Russian Olive hedge.
She said no at first, then yes.
He said in a slow sentence
the great painter should not
scuff around in unpolished shoes.
He oiled & polished her worn flats,
they shined, slick, like new.

September, 1973

7

O'Keeffe empties the sleeve
of her Chinese coat of fuzz
"My opinion is not worth much"
I pick the fuzz off her coat.
We walk round the driveway
in Abiquiu, so many times
make a mile, the light faded,
she gestures to the mesa
behind the house, "Let's go in now.
The magic is gone.
It will be chilly soon."
We lock all the doors together.

September, 1973

8

Light supper at Abiquiu
with O'Keeffe
in the dining room
adobe painted white.
She said the room is white
so she can see
more easily.

November, 1973

9

O'Keeffe listening to Richter
playing the Schumann
Piano Concerto
Sitting still
eyelids closed
occasionally recrossing
a leg.
One painting
rock on a stump
with clouds
on west wall of studio;
south wall, a painting
with black V
white below
blue above. Of that one painting
she said it was
what she was trying
to do
but the public
liked other things
that she didn't.

November, 1973

10

Looking at a photograph
of the house at Lake George
O'Keeffe remembered having
a porch taken off
for more light.
Stieglitz didn't like it
because she did it
without asking
anyone.

November, 1973

11

O'Keeffe said
when she first came
to this area
around Abiquiu,
didn't notice
houses along the river
because the land
is so huge,
studio window full
of sky,
stars,
cliffs.

December, 1973

12

Evening at Abiquiu
listening to Pachelbel's *Canon*
in the studio at the desk
O'Keeffe arranged and
rearranged five dark smooth rocks
changing their position on the
white table with the music.

December, 1973

13

O'Keeffe had a metal bell
at Ghost Ranch that rang
in a slight wind—
so whatever she said or did
seemed most special
when that bell sounded.

March, 1974

14

O'Keeffe was not enthused about
women's lib. "If the women screaming
about inequality would go home
and get on with their business
there would be no problem."
She always had to stretch her canvases
better, paint better, and make a better
show than the boys; not the men
—the boys—she said just a few
liked her work; she could have been stopped
at any point; she was pleased when she got
a headline, any headline, good or bad,
no matter. If she was not on top,
then she wanted out.

March, 1974

15

O'Keeffe said she painted in the car
driver's seat of a Model-A
unbolted and turned around,
windows tall and perfect,
wore an old wool skirt with elastic
around the waist; O'Keeffe put her clothes
into that skirt, tied one end,
balanced it on her head and walked
til she found a place to rest.
She was brown all over she said.
If while she was painting someone came up,
O'Keeffe said she had a dress
to wrap around and fasten in front.
She remembered this lying in the sun
dressed in black on the banco.

March, 1974

16

O'Keeffe said
men didn't like her colors
and the subjects she chose,
"But, no mind—I would
probably have a closet full right
now if no one had cared
for my work."
Her early years
were the best
because she was surrounded
by people who didn't care.
She was free.

March, 1974

17

I worked for O'Keeffe at first
as librarian in the book room.
It smelled of old paper
sweet, sharp, and dusty
bare bulb overhead
plywood table
books all over
on the floor, in crates
on shelves, in boxes.
I listed these books
cataloged them
on a manual typewriter
sitting on a cane bottom chair.
Is this how a medieval scribe felt?
To relieve my hours
she hung a small painting
on the west wall,
brilliant scarlet poppies.
Asked her after lunch,
"May I have that little painting?
Will you give it to me?
I like it." She snorted
didn't laugh
didn't say anything

She snorted. . . loudly
Years later
looking at a paper
for an auction
I learned how much
money it was worth.
She snorted at me
there in the library.
Turned
went out the door.

March, 1974

18

O'Keeffe in the book room
remembered Stieglitz grabbing
a book off a shelf
standing there reading it
as if his life depended on it.

March, 1974

19

At Lake George
on the table
where Alfred wrote
O'Keeffe
had the habit
of arranging
a dish with mosses
leaves and little plants
from the forest.
Stieglitz worked
facing the window
where he would often
see a cloud
rush out
to photograph it.

April, 1974

20

O'Keeffe spoke of stretching canvas
for a cloud painting 26 ft. x 8 ft.
from original 2-inch sketch
lost in the initial stages,
rubbing her hands palm to palm,
her long fingers bending and unbending
describing the anxiety, smoothing
her napkin to show a stretching
technique with the canvas.
Huge roll of canvas
she could barely lift.
Frank, an Abiquiu sheepherder,
real hard worker
helped her with heavy work,
they spread the canvas
on the garage floor over paper
to "let it rest"—didn't know
why a canvas needs to rest
before stretching,
does better when you let it
lie awhile for two to three days.
She and Frank set grommets around edges
built a frame reinforced with steel,
laced canvas onto the frame,
Frank tightened, strained

then tacked the canvas.
O'Keeffe watched.
To paint the 26-foot painting—sky and clouds
O'Keeffe stood on two 10-foot-long tables
then one 6-foot plank, sat on the table,
then stood on a chair, then sat on a chair,
then on the floor to reach all parts
of the canvas; any coat of color
must cover the whole canvas in a day
because there would be a line
where she stopped.
Frank would come
to the ranch, mix huge amounts of paint
for her in the morning. She rose at six,
painted all day, found herself cleaning
brushes at 9 pm; took two months.
A girl from Abiquiu cooked for her.

April, 1974

21

Breakfast with O'Keeffe
fresh sliced fruit, fresh orange juice
Jasmine tea or fresh coffee
hot chili with oil
marinated with garlic
in the fridge overnight;
maybe eggs soft-boiled
or scrambled, to your taste,
the bread a meal itself
whole wheat and soy flour,
wheat germ, ground flax seed,
sunflower seeds, and butter
mixed with safflower,
then savory jam maybe
ginger and green tomato
or sweet raspberry.
One day she said
what do you write about me?
Are you going to tell
what I eat for breakfast?

April, 1974

22

Near the Abiquiu graveyard
on a walk before supper
O'Keeffe pointed out the morada
sanctuary of the Penitentes.
From Jemez mountains a rider rushed
on a white stallion, stopped there
rearing before us
hooves pawing, loud neigh
rider just holding him.
I stood in front of O'Keeffe
waving my arms to protect her.
Later O'Keeffe scolded me
said she was more practical
had checked the barbed wire fence
to roll under it in her black dress.

April, 1974

23

Easter morning with O'Keeffe
we got up at 2 am, dressed warmly,
ate light breakfast in the kitchen,
toast and juice, then put on
long black wool cape she lent me
rode in back of Volkswagen van
past Ghost Ranch along a dirt road
curving and bumpy from spring melt.
She sat still. I braced myself
against the wall and roof of the van.
O'Keeffe said, "Sometimes you must
just sit like a sack of potatoes."
At Christ in the Desert Monastery
we walked into a dark sanctuary
sweet with incense. One
father asked, "Are you her daughter?"
We sat to the right for hours
in the cold on a hard bench
sometimes standing, listened
to Spanish and Latin,
watched candles; followed chanting

light slowly coming on red cliffs.
We walked out at sunrise
bright open space with river
immense cliffs, many people talked
with O'Keeffe, we ate, drove home,
slept the rest of the day.

April, 1974

24

O'Keeffe talked
of Macchu Picchu
where she spent three days.
Orchids grew within a few yards
of the door of the place
where she stayed. Being cautious
of snakes she let the blooms alone.
"They just sat out there and looked at you."

April, 1974

25

O'Keeffe looked sad and tired
from working on her book,
said she didn't care
if she lived or died;
One friend measured her to see
if she'd fit in narrow 7-foot black box
holding sheets and towels
in the studio—the friend said,
"It would do; but what a waste
of a fine box." When she laughs
O'Keeffe has pink cheeks.

April, 1974

26

Ghost Ranch household settling down.
Curtains open for O'Keeffe
to enjoy stars and moonlight.
Medicine is given, doors locked.
Jingo the chow on guard in the patio.
We listen to Ashkenazy playing
Beethoven piano Sonata "Appassionata"
O'Keeffe has five records of artists playing
that piece, she listens eyes closed.

April, 1974

27

Last Saturday at lunch
O'Keeffe said she read
good many articles about women
accomplishing much in sports
beating records
going faster and longer.
She thought it was a mistake
for women to tip their hand,
"We can act weak and sick
and female—all the while
knowing secretly
we are very strong."

June, 1974

28

O'Keeffe sitting on low adobe wall
Gazing at Truchas peaks east of Abiquiu.
Mosquitoes land on her
but don't bite,
walk along her thin wrinkled arm and fly off.
She says B vitamins & garlic.

September, 1974

29

After supper on our walk to the cliffs
O'Keeffe remembered Ida Rolf in New York
used to come twice a week, 9 am,
massage her, leave her feeling
like she was walking on air,
called Rolf "The big horse"
rather large strong woman.
Ida Rolf used to pick up her pelvis
with just her fingertips, special talent
most people do not have.
O'Keeffe said she owed everything
she ever did—to Ida Rolf.

September, 1974

30

O'Keeffe remembered Charles
who taught her to drive, showed her
Ghost Ranch for the first time.
Up the road from river valley
she saw it, knew it was home.
For her walk a headdress of a black scarf
pulled back like an Arab or nun
shawl over short black silk kimono
fragile white blouse
with knots for buttons
loose long flannel black pants.

September, 1974

31

O'Keeffe teaching art in Texas
showed students
how to fill a square space
in a beautiful way
then a round space
how to address an envelope
with a beautiful touch.

September, 1974

32

One
knows
when
Miss
O'Keeffe
is
really
mad
she
doesn't
say
a
word.

September, 1974

33

Before lunch we walked to the cliff
at Ghost Ranch, O'Keeffe said she lived
through two wars and Stieglitz.
First went to his "291" gallery to see
what modern things were done in America
instead of museum examples of whatever
we seemed to be through with.

September, 1974

34

O'Keeffe said to me
many young lonely people
would come to her
to find out
how to make it
what method?
For the most part
they were bores.
What she could offer
was the knowledge
you just
have to work
very hard
in the right direction.
There is
no
secret
method.

October, 1974

35

O'Keeffe seated on a wooden folding chair
among piñon and juniper trees before the cliffs.
I sit on the ground, lean on a walking stick,
face her as a pupil at the foot of a sage.
We watch the sun set slowly and she says,
"Imagine, having someone help me with every
little step when I used to run up and down
here all the time, walk ten miles and not feel it."

October, 1974

36

O'Keeffe gestured to different parts
of cliffs at Ghost Ranch
her favorite places,
didn't go
where there were rocks
and most likely snakes
stuck to the good earth
where there were cliffs
like curtains
wandered & wandered
looking for
the base of the pillars
finally by accident decided to go
up an arroyo and found herself
at the base of the pillars.

October, 1974

37

Walked to cliffs
across clear blue sky
long fluffed-out ribbed
jet vapor trail curving.
O'Keeffe said
she would like to
make a pot
with that feeling
then explained how
to shell and crush
cardamon seeds.
Today I see more.

October, 1974

38

Yesterday evening
walking to red cliffs
O'Keeffe said she dreamed
of being a white bird
with huge wings
gliding in the air
then floating still
in the sky.
She said she had never seen
the kind of bird
she wanted to be.

October, 1974

39

This evening I drove O'Keeffe
to Echo Amphitheater west of Ghost Ranch.
She pointed out a huge Modigliani
in the cliffs—it amused her
because it was so enormous.
As we walked up close to the cliff
we came to a Douglas fir
growing at a slant from the trail,
O'Keeffe commanded, "Look at that tree!"
I looked, shouted, "Hello, O'Keeffe!" to echo.

October, 1974

40

Years back
in Abiquiu
O'Keeffe said
there was an
ornate roof
over a telephone
you had to
take your own
bulb to the place
screw it in
make your call
and carry it home.

October, 1974

41

O'Keeffe told me
about Eduardo
whose grandfather was
a Penitente in Abiquiu;
his straight up and down ears
no slant to them
she thought they were
elegant
studied them at length
sitting behind him
once in the church.
Grandfather would wake Eduardo
to see the morning star
started teaching him
Penitente songs, then quit.
Grandfather said
they were
too difficult.

October, 1974

42

Standing at the window
Ghost Ranch studio
looking north to cliff
maybe storm coming
smell of rain, big wind
low grey clouds rushing south
at sunset. I see something
floating there — great skull
huge above the cliffs in clouds.
I inhale deeply, Ah!
have I learned to see like O'Keeffe?
Is this my O'Keeffe vision at last?
then the truth — on the studio wall behind me
lit from below, a small spotlight
skull reflected in the picture window
reminds me of her painting
red hills, skull and hibiscus.
I sigh deeply — Ah!
O'Keeffe snoring in the next room.

October, 1974

43

In her years in New York
whenever she tried something new,
men around her predicted failure.
When O'Keeffe did the first
huge Jimson weed, Stieglitz bent
over it with a handkerchief
hanging from his lips.
Stieglitz was dropped
as a two-week-old baby
they didn't notice
the broken nose
he could only breathe
out of one nostril.
To get more air
he would fit
the very corner
of a handkerchief
between teeth
it would hang from his mouth
he would talk that way.
He had a very well-formed mouth,
leaned over Jimson weed painting and said,
"What do you intend to do with this?"
O'Keeffe replied, "I will just paint it."

Nothing new to her
someone predicting failure.
When I read to her
from *Secret of the Golden Flower*
about weak and inferior women,
she replied,
"It's just the boys writing."

October, 1974

44

Asked O'Keeffe
how to judge
reproductions of paintings.
She explained
you look
to have the feeling
reproduced, not
each color precisely
the same as the original.
Someone learning from another
was apt to try too hard
and miss the mark.
A number of young men
tried to do
what Stieglitz did
and tried too hard.

October, 1974

45

O'Keeffe remembered
Mabel Dodge Luhan in Taos
who knew Isadora Duncan
and wore chiffons
covering her ugly hands
would invite people over
sit in such a way
no one dared
say a word.
SILENCE.
O'Keeffe delighted
to come to the party
asking how everyone was
making noise
soon everyone relaxed
and carried on.
Then Mabel Dodge could not
say how stupid
the Taos crowd was.

October, 1974

46

Tony Luhan, Georgia, and Rebecca
lost in Navajo country
on logging trails
built a huge bonfire
for the night.
Rebecca & Georgia couldn't sleep
cleaned themselves with cold cream.
Tony was enchanted
with cold cream
there they sat
in the dark morning
before sunrise
smearing themselves
with cream.
O'Keeffe was
surprised Mabel Dodge
hadn't shown him
cold cream before.

October, 1974

47

O'Keeffe said she was a slave
to the Stieglitz clan
at Lake George
had to oversee
kitchen and grounds.
When she made noises about it,
life wasn't worth living.
Because there wasn't time
for her work, she began
traveling around to find
a place to be alone,
ended up out here
at Ghost Ranch
70 miles from Santa Fe
2,000 miles from Lake George.

October, 1974

48

O'Keeffe showed me a spot
up in Ghost Ranch, red hills
where I could find
one charred, petrified tree
gather good stones.
In another place
showed me an arroyo
where I can gather
smooth black shiny rocks.

October, 1974

49

O'Keeffe said,
"I knew Hirshhorn was coming one day
Knew exactly where he would sit
Put one black pot just out of reach.
When Hirshhorn arrived, he sat just where
I knew he would and glanced around.
When he looked at the pot,
he jumped back like it had stung him.
Acted like nothing had happened.
I didn't say anything.
After a while he reached over, pulled it
to him, looked at it, asked who made it.
I said someone in the valley
whose name I don't remember.
At first he said it looked like
an oriental pot, then as he
picked it up, looked at it all over
he said whoever made this
is a very sensitive person.
After a little while
he bought it.
He came
not wanting
to buy anything
but he bought it.

Some people
you have to fool."
—said she hadn't been
in the art world 50–60 years
for nothing.

October, 1974

50

Walking with O'Keeffe
in semi-arid desert
on dirt road by red hills.
The earth breathed,
the ground was fluid beneath my feet.
I walked on a gently rocking boat
amazed in orange air at sunset.
I said, "The land is alive."
She did not pause, did not glance,
did not stumble, stepped through swells
of breath upon rocking soil
sure of her old feet
she said, "Yes, men have not been here
to ruin it."

February, 1975

51

One Sunday morning walk to the cliffs
sky blue and a few clouds. O'Keeffe said
she has a difficult time
visualizing eternity, how can the sky
go on and on, said she wanted to be buried,
then didn't want anyone to think of her
buried up at Abiquiu by the house,
she would rather have her ashes
spread out by the cliffs where she can
become part of the grass and the trees,
another kind of eternity, kind of immortality,
said the grass out there
needs all the
help it can get.

May, 1975

52

Laura Gilpin doing a portrait of O'Keeffe
Laura 85 and O'Keeffe 89
O'Keeffe in the window at Abiquiu studio
holding her pot in various poses
asked Gilpin not to photograph her grinning
"All those grinning Americans.
You would think all we had was funny."
Miss Gilpin works quietly, takes a little time
with each pose, said after you do a shot,
funny how people will just drop
into the more natural pose.
Laura had thickened ankles and teetered on her feet
occasionally used a cane—Nikon 35mm
Kodak 3 1/4, said her work at Canyon de Chelly
got her started with 35mm, she would shoot
whatever she would come back to later,
that won her over, said time was she would never
have thought of doing such a job on anything
other than her box camera. But with her disability
she had to be prudent.

June, 1975

53

Killed a rattler on the patio yesterday
may have saved O'Keeffe's life.
She talked to Brenda in little bedroom
I carried yogurt and cookies along the portal.
On a mat in front of the screen door
2-foot-long snake coiled and rattling,
O'Keeffe started for the door
I shouted, "Stop! Snake! Don't come out!"
Brenda repeated for her to hear
O'Keeffe headed back through the bathroom
into the studio calling the chows
inside the big old door.
Brenda raced to her car and sped away.
O'Keeffe came to the patio
told me to kill the snake.
Told her I was vegetarian
didn't believe in killing.
O'Keeffe said if I didn't
she would. I said I would then
to save her from being bitten.
Little creature was behind the wood.
O'Keeffe handed me a shovel.
I banged around the wood pile.
Finally it crawled out under

sagebrush and I crashed down
with the shovel, feeling awful.
O'Keeffe cheering me on
from inside the studio
told me to dig a hole
burn the snake in it
cover it with dirt.
Otherwise the fangs
might poison the dogs
if they dug it up.
Felt weak and trembling inside
O'Keeffe gave me something to drink
went into the studio sat quietly listening
to Bach solo cello Sonata by Casals
Calmed down watching rich sunset;
O'Keeffe told of many snakes
she had killed around Ghost Ranch.
It was a regular occurrence
but she never got used to it.
We read two volume authority on
rattlesnakes, how to walk with a cane
and vibrate the earth so the snakes
feel you coming and move away.
Then we discovered one of the gates

left open a little, enough for a snake,
her snake gates had L-shaped sides
that closed snugly, snake fences went down
two feet into the ground, fine mesh,
her buffalo skull was stolen.
Robbers had left the snake gate open.
O'Keeffe said it was not unusual
for someone from the village
to flee when crisis occurred.

October, 1975

54

Today before I left
O'Keeffe held my hand
I felt the blood pumping
in her fragile hand.
She so small in the bed
covered with her black comforter
O'Keeffe, her quick looks
her plans, her rocks, her erect body
her voice early in the morning
her methodical napkin folding.
I braided her hair for bed.

October, 1975

55

Lunch at Ghost Ranch
O'Keeffe asked me, "Have you heard
of legal problems with people
very critically ill being taken
off medication & let die?"
I said, "My grandfather had that
happen just last week."
She said, "How will they tell
when people are just tired
of taking care of you?"

October, 1975

56

While we ate dinner
watched the sun finish itself
against the cliffs
one high place
far East held the sun
good long time.
O'Keeffe reminisced
about Stieglitz
how he merely ate zwieback,
toast, and hot chocolate
for breakfast, never another
meal until a large dinner
nervous stomach.
She tried for ten years
to eat that way
got very ill
then decided she didn't want to die
so there were two meals
one for him
another for her.

October, 1975

57

Dinner at Ghost Ranch: quelite soup
cheese, rice crackers, salad.
O'Keeffe showed me the secret
of her salad dressing: garlic
chopped into a large spoon
salt sprinkled over garlic
fresh tarragon and basil
mashed into it, olive oil poured
over, then lemon juice or vinegar
pour drippingly over dry greens
toss with the same spoon.
White, wide plates, white bowls,
white cloth, plain brown straw mats
salt in white salt cellars
shaped like hour glasses
tiny mother-of-pearl spoons.
On the stove for the soup spoon
little ashtray, gaudy purple, green, yellow
from O'Keeffe's favorite
restaurant in Madrid.

October, 1975

58

This afternoon we found
one unconscious hummingbird
had battered itself against
the studio window, took it
to the kitchen, made sugar water
carried it to the garden
it sipped and perked up alive
irridescent blue green chin
whirred off suddenly up.

May, 1976

59

O'Keeffe said "Starry Night"
(little squares of light on blue field)
was done on very cheap paper
you used for drawing class.
So cheap you started fires with it
and wrapped packages with it,
said she could paint freely
on such paper, where one had to be
very careful on watercolor paper
at $2.00 a sheet.

August, 1976

60

At lunch O'Keeffe said
Stieglitz used to rub
bee's wax over his photographs
to bring out the color
of the paper
bought thin sheets of it
melted it down
into a bucket
kept a shaving brush in it
heated it just a little
before applying it
to photographs.

August, 1976

61

Yesterday, went into the studio
5 ft. x 8 ft. canvas there
yellow-brown over white
patio door with tiles.
In another room on the backside
of a canvas, a large piece of paper
the same size with the same forms
sketched out in charcoal.
O'Keeffe in a chair,
feet propped up,
studying the work.
On the stereo—Caedmon
recording of Noh plays,
ancient male chanting sound,
had me check her brushes
to see if they were clean
four of them
different sizes and shapes.

August, 1976

62

O'Keeffe described a performance
by Wanda Landowska.
One man came on stage
carefully dusted the piano keys
tiny woman with a little waist
entered in black taffeta
looked as if
she had slept in it
dainty pointed slippers
like bedroom shoes.
Then this little lady
took out a handkerchief
meticulously dusted each key
brought down the house
"Be sure the piano keys
are clean!" O'Keeffe
played a record of Landowska
playing Bach
aggressive, passionate, loud, fast.
O'Keeffe said,
"Make the most
of your appearance,
make it a real performance."

August, 1976

63

O'Keeffe dressed in black suit
silver flower "OK" Calder pin
white scarf at her neck
hair in french roll at the back
felt like riding to the ranch
to get warm things
velvet hood,
quilted Chinese coat, gloves
kleenexes for watering eyes
talking about a critic
who said she was influenced
by Thoreau and Emerson.
"I'm supposed to have read
Thoreau as a child.
I don't remember that.
I don't remember anything
about him.
I have found
when something is written
which is untrue,
it is best
not to comment
because that only

draws attention to it.
Otherwise it disappears
and fewer people
notice it."

March, 1977

64

Read O'Keeffe some poetry
she said was interesting
but didn't remember much
wasn't good enough
writing about a pitiful
part of the world
that didn't amount
to much.
There is so much
that matters in the world.
She described a jade knife,
curving blade handle
that was something
one remembered.
It mattered.
This special life
in things
O'Keeffe likened
to wind.

March, 1977

65

O'Keeffe said
she used to have
a mirror on a bureau
when she grew up
had pink pansies
painted around the top frame.
In that mirror
her face seemed round.
When Stieglitz
began photographing her
she realized
that her face
is long.

March, 1977

66

Looking at photo print
of pelvis bone floating in sky
O'Keeffe said
she was seldom pleased
by what she painted
never reached what
she saw
what she intended.
She was amazed
people seemed to like
what she did
always felt
she must work on
try again.
If she ever reached
what she saw
she would
stop painting.

March, 1977

67

O'Keeffe says her success
isn't due to talent
so much as nerve
and hard, hard work
plus a sort of simplifying
deciding, limiting, giving up
some things in favor
of painting.
If she was up
all night dancing
she wouldn't paint
for three days at a time.
I remember her saying
to my friend at a meal
talking about his painting,
"Isn't it fun?"
When she works,
it's for a whole day at a time.
Goes into a rage
if anyone pampers her.
Walks, does rolfing exercises
reads the news, creates, eats carefully.
I want to give her a present
Jasmine tea, cheese,
candied ginger—maybe next week.

December, 1977

68

The long room
on north white wall an African mask
oval and black with protruding mouth
and slitty eyes; long braid
extending up from the head.
O'Keeffe said there were two,
but the other one was not so fine.
She used to take it with her summers
hang a painting next to it—
if it held its own
the painting was good,
next to the mask.

January, 1978

69

O'Keeffe chatted after lunch
warmed her back at the gas wall heater,
told me about Aunt Ollie who lived to 103
one of the first people O'Keeffe remembers
visiting as a child. Her O'Keeffe sister
fixed up Aunt Ollie with a housekeeper and nurse
before she got back home,
Aunt Ollie had fired
both of them.
If anyone gave Aunt Ollie vitamins,
she threw them under the bed.
O'Keeffe said that is the way
she herself was
when she was
a little girl
if horrible foul-tasting medicine
didn't suit her,
she would chuck it
under the bed.

January, 1978

70

O'Keeffe said a very old friend
of hers—Dave—was one of the few
people she could stand with
in a beautiful place
and feel all alone.
Those people are pretty rare
she said, she once stood
with him on the rim
of the Grand Canyon
and felt alone.

January, 1978

71

O'Keeffe described exercises
Ida Rolf gave her:
two knees to chest
one knee to chest
then the other, lying down,
move head back and forth
stretch neck with hands
bend both knees then lift
get off floor using only legs
first one side
then another
some stretches with arms
hands facing one way
then another
enterprising for
a ninety-year-old.
Asked me what I thought
if she lived to 100.

January, 1978

72

O'Keeffe's friend Mortimer
used to read Greek
kept a Greek book
by his bed
late in his years
lost his mind.
O'Keeffe said
it was very sad
he just wasn't there.
What O'Keeffe feared most
was going off her head,
losing her mind.

January, 1978

73

In the studio
on the white rug
leaning against the white bed
by the window
where I will sleep.
Just did the dishes
after a meal of leftovers
cold lamb, brie cheese, buttered bread,
warmed quelites, crab soup,
beer and mint tea.
Cold wind
moves skim of clouds
past the piece of moon
out there.
"Black Place" on the wall
in the studio here
over one
dramatic black pot.
On the long shelf
two grey paintings
with two even larger
black pots underneath.

February, 1978

74

Here again in the middle of beauty.
O'Keeffe in black met me at the gate
squeezed past the chows
helped her lift the gate to close it,
latch it, lock it.
She showed me into the big bedroom
where she had been painting
thick huge pieces of papers on the bed
large brushes and dishes,
sponges, aprons, cheesecloth,
spatters on tissue, thick mat board
cut thin across leaning against the wall
by the fireplace, test swatches of black,
grey, varying intensities, shades.
One three-part porcelain dish
a beautiful blue in it, somewhat dried
some sumi-e brushes and pens
with assorted tips, big tube of black
Mars Black Liquitex
she cleared things off when we came in
said if I felt
like doing anything literary
I could use that part of the desk.

I wouldn't hurt the paper
there is a good lamp there
I am sitting on a stool
drying my hair
my back to this fire.

January, 1978

75

Stopped to see what O'Keeffe
had been painting
in the large bedroom
on the table in the room
fragrant with oil paint
a white painted canvas
3 ft. by 2 ft.
patio door white on white,
white stones along the bottom
on the bed, resting,
large pieces of paper
with blue, black, and grey
watercolor calligraphic paintings
one a bluish curl
stretch of paint,
one a grey and black circle
within a circle
down to a center,
another a grey circle
with a cross inside.
I was tempted to look closely
but felt too intrusive,
left to bask
in the sun.

March, 1978

76

I was sitting on top
of the patio well
in the sun
facing the black door.
O'Keeffe came
through the passage
under the Japanese shell wind chimes
back from the garden
where she supervised
two men from the village
her black suit
sturdy brown leather shoes
rosewood cane and tan gloves
grey-black hair
twisted at the nape
of her neck
dignity of many years
if slightly uncertain step
past the black door
up the steps
down the passage toward the studio.
She stopped and mused
over the damp patch

of mud in the wall
where the Mayan face
had been stuck
but fell out.
She wondered aloud
where they put the face.

March, 1978

77

Sunday morning O'Keeffe and I
discussed how to find your own voice,
your own vision.
I argued a painter can get off
alone and work in color
but a writer must use words
which requires a community
of minds, you write to a community
of minds, I said.
She spoke harshly, very loudly,
"Do you think that
community of minds cares a moment
for what you have to say?
Of course they don't!"
She answered herself.
She said I was writing
like others told me
said it was a very difficult
thing to listen to yourself
and write from that
said the key is free time.
Give yourself an hour or two a day.

all to yourself
everyone has free time
but they don't use it
I said I have time when I am walking
to school—she said that wasn't free
yes I was walking, but I was walking to—
that wasn't free time.

March, 1978

78

O'Keeffe said, "This is the last meal
we will have together."
I said, "Yes, for this trip"
possibility of immanent death
outlined everything distinctly
from everything else
for some moments I noticed many details
about her gestures
her clothes, her jaw chewing.
Saturday, watched her sleep
in warm sun
Sunday after lunch we sat
on a bench in the sun
back to back
white down pillow
between us
a honey bee buzzed my
underarms and face
our heads and upper backs touching
she wore a floppy straw hat.

March, 1978

79

Frightens me to think of
O'Keeffe dying
just walked into the studio
sat in white covered chair
opposite the bed
where she is sleeping
dressed in black
—blue shoes—
brown soft wooly coverlet
woven from chow dog fur
over her legs
grey hair blends with white pillow
deep window sill behind her
with gracefully curved
long horns
and beyond all that
the land—the emptiness.

April, 1978

80

In O'Keeffe's bedroom
on the wall by the fireplace
attached to the dark brown wall
one very composed right hand
of a Buddha
given Miss O'Keeffe
by Richard who lives near Taos
with his Arabian horses.
Last night she told me
it used to be broken
and one of the middle fingers
would move
back and forth.
She sent it to be fixed
when it returned
a special something it had was lost—gone
now it's just a hand.
It had a patina on black
like lacquer or enamel
slightly upturned fingers
seems the hand of a blessing
palm outward
long long fingers
like Miss O'Keeffe's.

April, 1978

81

I walked slowly carefully
to O'Keeffe dressed in black
sitting on a log near the cliffs
kneeling beside her
played a few notes on my flute
she said my playing
reminded her of walking
in mountains of Peru
where boys would come
out of nowhere
playing their high flutes
she reminisced how she drove
a station wagon up to the cliffs
just beyond where we were sitting
slept several nights
in the back
where she could get up early,
make breakfast,
immediately start painting.
After sitting awhile
we quietly walked
back, discussing the direction
of the cool wind.

April, 1978

82

This time I brought O'Keeffe
a pineapple and an Ikebana arrangement
of mums, eucalyptus and purple flowers
she said it looked like it grew there
on the wall over black linen box
Black Place painting
and black charcoal
aerial view of a river.
On the table Metropolitan *Steichen*
Masterprints 1895–1914.
At the head of the bed
on the floor
folded up bear skin.
On the wide north window sill
3-foot-high sprawling bent over
Blood of Christ plant
bright red blooms on branching tips
behind me on the sink
a one-inch vase, a black one
with tips of two slim
pointed green leaves,
one tipped yellow
sticking out
of the narrow top.

April, 1978

83

O'Keeffe talked about a dog
blind in one eye, missing a paw
real gentleman dog that used to
hang out by her back door
follow her around when he could.
Once the dog followed her down
across the highway to Bode's General Store
she started back up the hill and noticed
he wasn't following
looked down at the highway
saw his crushed body
a semi had passed so fast
on the dog's blind side
he didn't see it.
She went up to get Estiben
they put the dog in a wheelbarrow
cried all the way up the hill.

May, 1978

84

O'Keeffe remembered
running away from home
as a small girl.
She had forgotten why
she was angry at the folks,
and decided to leave
remembered walking
down the road thick with trees
on either side
at the end of the road
a bright red sun
setting between the trees
she had a feeling
she was walking
into the sun
she will never forget
that feeling.
Her memory reminded me
of the watercolor
she's been working on
in Claudia's big bedroom.
"Yes, but it doesn't come close
to what I feel, what I felt
that day I was running away."

May, 1978

85

O'Keeffe had a small tent
that was orange
and thin
and lightweight
if you awoke
on a moonlit night,
seemed like twilight
all night
or like sitting
in a glowing fireplace.
There was a flap
you could open
and watch the stars.

May, 1978

86

O'Keeffe remembered the Gaspé
with Georgia Engelhart learning to drive.
They came down a steep incline
without changing gears for a sharp turn
at the bottom of the grade and they quarreled.
Got out of the car & started walking
really very dangerous because everyone
had a bearskin tacked to the wall.
They walked along the steep road
to one side wall of fir trees
so thick you couldn't walk through them.
There was a sign just as they almost turned back.
It read, "Road to the sea
seals and birds of all kinds,"
O'Keeffe said it was
one of the most beautiful places
she has ever seen in her whole life
little cottage on the beach
with a supply of food.
Two huge waterfalls. One fell
into a spray on a mossy place,
a place with hot pebbles.
They had bunk beds,
though she never slept
because it was so beautiful.

They would paint awhile then walk.
She would be out ranging around
to see the place at night
in the moonlight.
One high flat rock where you could
lie on your belly and view
seals swimming below.
After three days she told Georgia E.
they would have to leave the place
so she could get some sleep.
O'Keeffe remembered at Lake George
they would take out
into the woods,
walk for miles without clothes.

May, 1978

87

O'Keeffe said
the red barn
she recently painted
came to her
in a dream,
the only painting
that she dreamed
first.

July, 1978

88

Driving Allen Ginsberg and Peter Orlovsky
to Ghost Ranch to meet O'Keeffe.
Deep blue cloudy sky
yellow paper flapping on the kitchen door
Allen went into the bathroom,
"To take a shit," he said
Peter drank two glasses of water
one from Jemez Mountain water at Abiquiu
in a glass jar, other from the tap
at Ghost Ranch house
"There is a difference," he said.
Peter went into the patio
among the sage
examined a number of rocks
she has arranged
on bancos and low benches
and tables. He would turn a rock
or a geode around and around
deeply sniff it
three or four times.
He said, "Did she do peyote?"
Allen came out of the bathroom
we walked around the potting shed
toward the cliffs.
Jingo & Inca, two chows across

the arroyo, woofing & snorting
beyond the low trees
O'Keeffe crosses the road with her cane,
"Well, did you get the raspberry juice
and crushed ice ready?" looked to me
O'Keeffe said to Ginsberg,
"Is she of any use to you?"
He replied, "I think she's
getting used to us now."

July, 1978

89

South porch of Ghost Ranch house
Allen Ginsberg sits with O'Keeffe
shows her how he meditates,
crossed legs, straightened back, closed eyes—
breathe slowly, other instructions
but she doesn't mimic him.
He asked, "What do you believe?"
She outstretched her arm
palm up in a semi-circle
in front of her toward Pedernal,
"It's hard to say."
Mountain to the south
fragrant sage, clouds, blue sky
rocks she had gathered
beauty around her everywhere.
Later driving Allen & Peter to Santa Fe.
Allen called her a witch.
I nearly drove
off a curve in the road.
Said he was surprised
how little money she had.
I explained simple
surroundings did not
show her wealth.
No need.

July, 1978

90

As bells for Santa Rosa day rang
O'Keeffe & I walked
through her "first rate garden"
walked out from the patio
with the black door
through the corridor with Japanese
shell chimes & garden tools.
She said for me to go first
because she is slower.
Walked a circle through the plants
picking flowers, a five-petaled
wonder she doesn't recognize,
herbs for lunch
lovage, tarragon, basil, dill,
asked me to choose
largest of a dozen eggplants
ripening so she could reach down
and hold it.
She chatted briefly with Estiben
weeding by the cilantro plot.
She carried her cane
walked carefully
as if in the dark
in a place she knows.

This evening we sat
in early night air.
For a while
she couldn't spot
the evening star.

August, 1978

91

Abiquiu studio 10 am,
O'Keeffe seated by the phone
in her blue dress
like a loose summer coat.
White shawl
around her shoulders
over her lap,
over most of her legs.
Hair covered
with thin white cotton scarf
pinned back like an Arab.
I sat on a black stool
presented a sack of bread.
She seemed pleased,
"We like to have you come
and cook for us."
Huge painting above
to her right on east wall
seemed about 6 ft. by 6 ft.
I said, "Wow," and inhaled.
She said I was to be impressed.
They took all morning
to hang it—the workman thought
he had done
a full day's work.

It was what she saw
one day from an airplane,
long floor of clouds
that extended
to the horizon
high sky blue
then greeny blue
then band of green light
then all white bottom half
in broad strokes
tiny white frame,
spacious & light.
It carries this room.

August, 1978

92

Last night O'Keeffe and I sat
in her studio by the phone.
She was dressed in white robe
hands folded looking content
white & grey hair
in a swoop in back
caught by grey comb
large grey hair pins
showed me unbound version
of Metropolitan book of
photographs of her by Stieglitz.
The Met will put out an issue in a box
and Viking an issue without a box.
Laughing, she told me
Metropolitan Museum
made huge banners
the size of her studio
three of them
to hang outside the Met
with huge letters saying,
"Georgia O'Keeffe by Alfred Stieglitz"
She wondered if she
went through life
like anyone else
would she get bored?

Mused what Alfred would do
if he saw those huge banners,
He would probably stand there thinking
looking up at the banner
with the handkerchief
hanging from his teeth.
He would say,
"So the world has
come to this?"

October, 1978

93

O'Keeffe said there was a Dutch physicist
one of those who worked with Einstein.
He wanted Stieglitz and her
to raise his 13-year-old daughter.
They came to a meal one day.
The girl copied what Stieglitz did
thinking it was important.
Stieglitz was absent-minded,
apt to put his coffee cup
beside the saucer
which the girl copied.
O'Keeffe had to explain.
She and Stieglitz
didn't take on raising
the little girl.
The wife taught
something in Russia
every other season
so they didn't have
much of a home.
There was an autistic son,
just a vegetable
in an institution.
Before World War I

the man took the son out
and killed him
then shot himself.
It left a mark on O'Keeffe.
She has told this story
to me before.

March, 1979

94

Noon meal Sunday
with O'Keeffe
looking out to
roofless room
toward red stone
in the niche
like auricles & ventricles
of a heart.
In the passage
to the garden
Japanese shell wind chimes
play in the breeze.
In the dining room
brown wooden Buddha
surrounded by
smooth stones
carefully placed.
O'Keeffe tapping
her plate with fork
and knife while eating,
careful attention
to what we eat
how we eat
chewing thirty times.

April, 1979

95

Just gave O'Keeffe
her morning yogurt
at 10:45
after reading to her
from *Book of Tea*
about an hour.
She is very sleepy
resting under her black quilt
with white wool cover
on top of her made up bed.
We have been reading
Eliot Porter's *Antarctica*
because the Porters
are coming for a meal
in a week.

April, 1979

96

This morning
O'Keeffe reminisced
about planting chrysanthemums
with young Jackie Suazo
in the garden.
When they finished,
she said
they must pray
over the plants
so they will grow.
She laughed
remembering
he looked at her
as if her prayer
wouldn't matter much
since she wasn't much use
to God on earth.

April, 1979

97

O'Keeffe remembered climbing
onto a meat block
with girlfriends
then jumping off.
She was appalled
at a friend
Leah
who jumped off,
skirts flying,
with nothing underneath.
O'Keeffe always
wore underwear
and there was Leah,
all free underneath.

April, 1979

98

O'Keeffe in the studio
fragrance of turpentine
Pachelbel's *Canon in D*
she wears midwest
farm woman's apron
tiny patterns
pink, red, blue
with yellow rick-rack.
Massive painting on easel
eight-foot-tall
upward black shapes
city buildings
blurry starlight circles
on west wall
waves of blue in sky
another easel—blue sky
grey monolith
everywhere looking.

May, 1979

99

Last evening
I commented
to Miss O'Keeffe
a large piece
of white watercolor
paper
looked particularly good
with rough surface
and curly edges.
She said,
"Yes, it'll never look
so fine
after something
is drawn on it."

May, 1979

100

Japanese poet
Nanao visits O'Keeffe
prepares her evening meal
hijiki seaweed
vegetables and eggs
salted while cooking
so it tastes sweet.
She is most interested
in his comment
about meditators today
the young ones
seem almost dead,
one must sit in quiet
but also
must be burning inside.

May, 1979

101

O'Keeffe has been reading
Jade Mountain, Chinese poems
translated by Witter Bynner
said she liked them so much
because each one
is a picture.
She thought
it had something
to do with the fact
they were written
by brushwork.
She has learned
from reading legal depositions
you must know *exactly*
what you mean
by each word.
You mustn't suppose
or imagine.
You must know.
For most of modern poetry
she says,
"It's for the birds."
I said *Jade Mountain*
made my work
look pretty pale.

She replied emphatically,
"Oh no! You are writing
for your time.
They wrote for their time
lucky not to have anyone
before them
to be writing like."

May, 1979

102

Weeks back we went
into the bookroom
to replace
Mayers's *Materials of the Artist*
stumbled upon
unbound portfolio
of *Ching Ming Chang Ho*
series of reproductions
of a thirty-foot
Chinese scroll
introduced at the Met
by her friend Alan Priest.
She spread it out
on the bed
where I sleep and
with her magnifying glass
looked at plate after plate.
said it was remarkable
an artist could
maintain that style
for so long,
curious where the outhouses were
for so many people
along the river and road,
listened as I read

about each plate
found things told about in writing
seemed interested
in the shape of bridges
size of cart wheels
bigger than people,
the shapes of the sails.

July, 1979

103

O'Keeffe remembered
when Stieglitz
first did
photographs
of her hands.
They were walking
up Fifth Avenue,
there was a screen
with hands.
No one would have thought
of doing hands like that
before Stieglitz's
portraits of her hands.

July, 1979

104

Earlier today
brushing and dressing
O'Keeffe's fine hair
into a french roll
with a figure "8"
at the top of her head.
She was talking
with Mino Lopez
Pita's brother
asking what he thought
of the black on the painting
they had worked on together.
He thought it too shiny.
She agreed
something must be
done about the black.
O'Keeffe said
he might have to sand it off
try again.
Mino wanted
to go to the fiesta
in Española
so wasn't interested
in staying past the time
to put the shine

on fresh wax
in the pantry and kitchen.
O'Keeffe said to me
she could make a painter
of Mino in a few years.
He has been dreaming
about painting.

July, 1979

105

O'Keeffe remembered a trip
to Vienna with Richard
who knew the man
managing the Lipizzans
so they always
got choice seats.
When the show began,
a man on a large stallion
rode in front of them
had the stallion rear up.
She was astonished
to see herself
beneath the stomach
of a big white stallion,
afraid it would land
right in her lap.

July, 1979

106

O'Keeffe cautious at the screen
of the studio, calling out,
"Carol?" in a husky high voice,
wearing gauzy kimono
embroidered white on white cotton
three or four large flowers.
I carried books, suitcase, purse
sack of peaches and pecans.
Stepped in, looked to the south wall
to see what was on display.
On her shelf,
flanked on the left by the sink
on the right thick boxes of records
Schnabel, Schubert, Monteverdi
Hayden, Beethoven, Vivaldi, Mozart, Bach.
One of the large grey paintings from
a Washington Monument series.
In front a strong white sculpture
of round forms and curls.

July, 1979

107

O'Keeffe described
getting lost
on the Texas prairie
with Claudia
out walking
near Palo Duro Canyon.
If you leave the depression
of the rutted road
only acres & acres
of grassland
no landmark
nothing to guide you.
Couple of times
pretty well frightened
by that experience.
You keep walking,
try to retrace your steps
but the soil
and grasses
don't hold
your footprints.
She said eventually
you come upon
a road
and you're not

lost anymore.
I asked if you could
follow the lights from town.
She laughed and said
that's when she really noticed
the evening star.
That's when she painted it,
a reassurance to see that light
shining even before
the sun went down.

July, 1979

108

O'Keeffe in white coat dress
at the studio sliding door
with red chow dog Jingo.
She said, "Let's get this over with."
I said,
"Good-bye,"
shook her hand.
She said,
"Good-bye."
I said, "See you next time."
She said,
"Good-bye."
I left by the big gate.
Last time I saw her.
She simply stood there
in the evening light.

July, 1979

This book is set in *Electra* designed
by W. A. Dwiggins *(1880–1956)* in 1935.
Early modernist with a rationalist axis,
this face has distinct clarity, yet through
its mix of thick and thin strokes
vim, snap, and sparkle.

Ornamentation is from *Caravan*,
also designed by Mr. Dwiggins.